Towers of Stone

The Story of English Castles

by Joanne Mattern

MODERN CURRICULUM PRESS

Pearson Learning Group

I magine living in a home built of thick, heavy stones. This home has no windows, just gaps in the stone to let in light and air—and bugs, rain, and cold. Heavy iron gates protect the entrance of this home. A strip of water, called a *moat,* surrounds the house to keep enemies from reaching it.

Hundreds of years ago, some people lived in homes just like this. These homes were called castles. They were not as comfortable as the houses we live in today. But they were designed to protect the people who lived in them.

The first castles were built about one thousand years ago. The lord, or ruler of an area, built a castle for protection against invading armies. These early castles were made of wood. A lord would build his castle on a hill surrounded by a ditch. The ditch was filled with water to create a moat. For added protection the castle was also surrounded by a strong fence called a *palisade* (pal-i-SAYD). Archaeologists have found the remains of many of these simple castles.

During the tenth century, English lords began building castles of stone. Stone towers were stronger than wooden ones, and they would not burn. Also, many people thought that stone castles were much more beautiful than wooden ones.

Stone castles were expensive and took a long time to build. A carver, known as a stonemason, would cut the stone into blocks. Then the blocks were carried to the site where the castle was being built. All this work had to be done using simple tools. Workers did not have the powerful machinery we use today!

Can you imagine the number of stones that were needed to build a castle? Early records show us how much work was involved. Windsor Castle, near London, England, is still used as a home by the British royal family. Windsor Castle was first built in 1086, but over the years it was rebuilt and improved several times. In 1365, a carver named Henry le Smythe split 156,200 stones for a building project at Windsor. In addition, a forest of six hundred oak trees was cut down for wood to be used inside the building.

During the mid-1300s, a new type of castle was built. This kind of castle had several rings of stone walls around it. It was well designed for defense against an enemy. If an army managed to break through the outer wall, it still had one or more inner walls to get through. And while soldiers battled along the outer wall, rows of archers could fire deadly arrows from the top of the inner wall.

The main entrance to a castle was usually protected by a heavy iron gate. This gate could be quickly lowered to seal off the castle during an attack.

As more castles were built, the shape of the towers also changed. Early towers were square.

Later towers were round. The architecture of a round tower makes it stronger than a square one. So, it was harder for an army to knock down a round tower and people inside had more protection. Round towers have a more graceful look too.

The part of the castle inside the walls was called a courtyard. This large, open space held many buildings. It had stables, where horses were kept. There were also workshops where craftspeople made goods such as iron pots and horseshoes. The courtyard was almost like the main street of a small town. People enjoyed meeting and talking in the courtyard.

The castle itself had many rooms. The most important was the great hall. The great hall was where people gathered to eat and conduct business. This was a colorful place. The walls were sometimes painted in bright colors or decorated with woven tapestries. These tapestries often showed scenes of heroes and battles. They not only brightened up the stone walls but also kept out drafts and made the great hall warmer.

During the day, the hall was filled with long tables where people ate. The day started early, with a simple breakfast of bread. The main meal of the day was around eleven o'clock in the morning. Supper was eaten early in the evening.

Almost everyone who lived in the castle was present during these meals. The lord and other important members of the court ate at the front of the room. Their table was often raised up on a platform. Other members of the household ate at tables set up in rows around the hall. The more important you were, the closer you sat to the lord's table.

Some suppers featured entertainers. Minstrels played music and sang. Jesters performed tricks and told jokes. After supper, the tables were moved out and simple straw mattresses were laid on the floor for the people to sleep on.

Far beneath the great hall, in the deepest darkest part of the castle, was the dungeon. The dungeon held prisoners. Dungeon cells were usually small, cramped, and damp. Often there was barely enough room for a prisoner to lie down. Food and water were passed through an iron door in the wall, or dropped through an iron grate in the ceiling. A person could end up in a dungeon for committing any crime or displeasing his lord. Many people died in these miserable places.

Other prisoners were kept in more comfortable cells in other parts of the castle. These prisoners were usually wealthy enemies who had been captured in battle. The lord often held these prisoners until their families could ransom them, or win their release by paying a large sum of money.

As time went on, castles became more elaborate. They were not only armed fortresses, but also comfortable homes for lords and their families. Instead of sleeping in the great hall with the soldiers and workers, the lord and his family built separate living quarters above the hall. These quarters featured bedrooms, a room to receive guests and important visitors, and *privies*, or primitive bathrooms.

The outside of the castle also became more elaborate. Carvers made intricate patterns in the stone. Sometimes intricate designs and statues were added to the walls.

One of the world's most famous castles is the Tower of London. This complex features several towers, a green, or enclosed square, and thick stone walls, sturdy enough to walk on. When a mason built a stone wall, he sometimes scratched his mark in the wall. Then he could count up the marks to see how much money he was owed. Today this castle is a museum visited by thousands of tourists, and many of the mason's marks are still visible. But it was once a fortress and prison where many unfortunate victims met their deaths.

Many famous people were held as prisoners at the castle. One, a church bishop named Ranulf Flambard, was sent there soon after the building was completed. Flambard was one of the luckier prisoners. He had a rope smuggled to him. Then he used the rope to climb down from one of the top floors and escape to freedom.

The heart of the Tower of London is the White Tower. It was built by William the Conqueror, a Frenchman, shortly after he invaded England in 1066. William built many castles around England to protect his new kingdom. Many English people did not want William to be their king and wanted to fight battles against him. William knew that building strong fortresses and castles was a good way to show his strength and protect himself against violence.

The man responsible for the White Tower's architecture was a monk named Gundulf. Like William the Conqueror, Gundulf was from France. He was quite famous as a designer of both churches and fortresses. For the White Tower, Gundulf designed a fortress that would dominate the city.

Gundulf's tower featured thick walls made of limestone brought from France. The high walls were pierced by arrow slits—narrow openings where archers could shoot arrows without being struck themselves. The walls were topped by four towers. Three were square and one was round. The building was 118 feet by 107 feet and was whitewashed to make it stand out even more. This whitewash is what gave the White Tower its name.

The main floor of the tower held a great hall, a sword room, and a chapel. Below this level were the barracks where soldiers lived. Above the main level was a chamber where the king held important meetings.

The White Tower was completed in 1078. After a storm damaged it in 1091, William the Conqueror's son, William Rufus, made many repairs. In the decades that followed, other kings made the tower even bigger and stronger.

The Tower of London remained the home of kings and queens until 1529. By then, Henry VIII was king. He preferred to live in a different castle called Hampton Court. Then the Tower took on a new role—that of a prison.

Henry VIII had many enemies, and he was quick to punish them by locking them up in the Tower. Most of these prisoners were noblemen or religious figures, so they were not kept in damp, crowded dungeons. Instead, these men and  women often had comfortable apartments, with fine furniture, collections of books, good food to eat, and even servants to wait on them. The only thing they did not have was their freedom. Henry also locked up two of his six wives in the Tower. Both of them were killed there.

The Tower served as a prison through the early 1600s. But by 1660, the Tower was abandoned and in poor condition. Then King Charles II improved the Tower and made it safe and secure once again.

By the middle of the eighteenth century, the Tower had become one of England's most popular tourist destinations. Now the Tower was known not only as a great fortress and prison, but also as a museum and the home of a zoo. Within its gates lived bears, wolves, tigers, lions, and an eagle. These animals were a great source of amusement to kings and queens and their guests, although the living conditions cannot have been very pleasant for the animals. The animals were often made to fight each other for sport, and were kept in cramped cages.

In addition to the zoo, the Tower also became home to the Royal Mint, the armories—a museum filled with suits of armor and weapons—and the crown jewels. The Mint was where England's money was kept. Official seals and medals were also crafted there. These medals and coins often featured intricate workmanship and ornamental designs. In the early 1800s, the Mint was moved to a separate building outside the Tower's grounds, but the armories and crown jewels remained.

In 1841, fire nearly destroyed the Tower of London. The fire began when a flue in one of the chimneys overheated. Within several hours, two towers and the armories were completely destroyed. Several other buildings, including the White Tower, were badly damaged. The heat was so intense that it melted the lead water pipes on the walls of the White Tower. The crown jewels were saved only because a brave policeman handed them out one piece at a time.

The Duke of Wellington, who was in charge of the Tower, saw the fire as an opportunity to rebuild the Tower and make it better than ever. He persuaded the British government to pay for the project. Within several years, all the towers had been rebuilt or repaired.

Today, the Tower of London remains one of the most popular tourist sites in the world. Visitors can walk along the walls and talk to the guards who patrol the grounds. They can visit the cells that held famous prisoners and see the graffiti these doomed men and women carved into the walls.

Most importantly, visitors can learn the history of the Tower. By walking through its halls, they can imagine what life was like hundreds of years ago. As they step across the stones of the Tower, or of any of England's ancient castles, they can reach out and touch the past.